Personal Branding in 2019

Strategies to Build Your Brand With Instagram, Facebook, Youtube and Twitter, Social Media Marketing and Network Marketing

Jack Gary

© Copyright 2019 by Jack Gary

All rights reserved.

The following Book is reproduced below with the goal of providing information that is as accurate and reliable as possible. Regardless, purchasing this Book can be seen as consent to the fact that both the publisher and the author of this book are in no way experts on the topics discussed within and that any recommendations or suggestions that are made herein are for entertainment purposes only. Professionals should be consulted as needed prior to undertaking any of the action endorsed herein.

This declaration is deemed fair and valid by both the American Bar Association and the Committee of Publishers Association and is legally binding throughout the United States.

Furthermore, the transmission, duplication or reproduction of any of the following work including specific information will be considered an illegal act irrespective of if it is done electronically or in print. This extends to creating a secondary or tertiary copy of the work or a recorded copy and is only allowed to express written consent from the Publisher. All additional right reserved.

The information in the following pages is broadly considered to be a truthful and accurate account of facts and as such any inattention, use or misuse of the information in question by the reader will render any resulting actions solely under their purview. There are no scenarios in which the publisher or the original author of this work can be in any fashion deemed liable for any hardship or damages that may befall them after undertaking information described herein.

Additionally, the information in the following pages is intended only for informational purposes and should thus be thought of as universal. As befitting its nature, it is presented without assurance regarding its prolonged validity or interim quality. Trademarks that are mentioned are done without written consent and can in no way be considered an endorsement from the trademark holder.

Table of Contents

Introduction 5
Chapter One: What is Personal Branding? 7
Chapter Two: An Introduction to Personal Branding in 2019 25
Chapter Three: Having the RIGHT Mentality to Build a Personal Brand 41
Chapter Four: How to Build a Personal Brand 64
Chapter Five: The Importance of Being Yourself 120
Chapter Six: Defining Your Audience 128
Chapter Seven: Personal Branding with Facebook 132
Chapter Eight: Personal Branding on Instagram 136
Chapter Nine: Personal Branding on YouTube 138
Chapter Ten: Personal Branding with Twitter 140
Chapter Eleven: Having Mentorships 142
Chapter Twelve: How to Monitor Your Personal Brand 146
Conclusion 151

Introduction

Many people in today's market have underestimated the power of the personal branding technique. There is a prevalent misconception that in order to achieve success in 2019 you have to be wildly exceptional and skilled beyond belief. However, every person has something unique to offer the world. The difference between whether they are successful or not lies not how skilled they are, and rather how well they package themselves and present their brands to the world. From Kim Kardashian to Martha Stewart, successful personal branding techniques have proven to be useful if not downright necessary to be a success today. Even for those who just wish to get a better job or specific opportunity, personal branding can still be used to set you apart from the crowd and better your efforts exponentially.

The following chapters will discuss proven tips and techniques for getting the best mindset to undertake your new endeavor, as well as an in-depth history and explanation of personal branding and why it is important. You will also find checklists and step by step guides to follow as you build your personal brand, as well as information on how to curate and manage accounts across social media. Finally, you will also find helpful examples of personal brands all throughout the book, as well as information on finding and securing mentorships and how to monitor your overall progress and success.

Chapter One: What is Personal Branding?

Most of us have probably heard of the term 'personal branding' before, right? Whether it was on the news, in a job-seeking self-help book, or even around the water cooler, it seems as though more and more people are talking about having a personal brand. So, what exactly *is* it? And more pressingly, why is it important?

A personal brand is essentially when people market their careers and titles, as well as their personalities and personas, as brands. This may be a big concept to grasp easily because it seems a bit ridiculous. How can a person be a *brand?* Let us take a moment to understand what a brand is. In the traditional sense, a brand is a uniquely named, uniquely designed entity that is used to sell a product or a chain of products. Brands are used to sell products and make money by creating an atmosphere around their logo and name that is associated with the positive aspects of whatever it is that they are selling. For example, one major brand most of us know and love is Nike, a company that produces athletic shoes and clothing. They have created a signature logo that many of us can recognize on the spot. They place that logo on everything they make to create a cohesive line of products that are recognizable as their own, as well as recognizable to others once consumers purchase their products and wear them in public, making them appear more popular and thus selling more products. They endorse famous athletes to create not only a wider branding image but a more 'high-end' one. If the most talented athletes use their products, they *must* be top of the line, right? They also ensure that the celebrities they endorse maintain a certain image themselves, one of dedication, pride, and sportsmanship, steering clear of other athletes who may be more troublesome so as to not affect the overall brand's image.

All of these things are done to create an overall feeling and impression among consumers about the brand. This is evidenced when you simply ask an average person to describe the brand using a few words. The common descriptors you'll hear are words like sleek, innovative, top of the line, and performance enhancing. You may even have respondents tell you how cool the brand is because *this* athlete or *that* celebrity wears them! So. You may be asking yourself right about now, "Ok, but does all of this have to with *personal branding?*" Well, personal branding is essentially the same process of maintaining a public image to sell a product. Only the product isn't a new pair of shiny sneakers or fuzzy wristbands. The product is you and your career. YOU are the uniquely designed, uniquely named entity that is used to make money, and you do not have to be a celebrity to do it. Your personal brand is an impression held by someone other than yourself that describes the experience of you and your relationship to others. To understand why personal branding is so important, you first have to understand the history of the personal branding concept.

Since mankind was first created, we have had to interact with others. And since we have had to interact with others, we have had to watch what we say and how we present ourselves. As time has moved rapidly forward, in today's world we now more than ever have seemingly endless areas in which we have to cultivate our personalities and how we interact with other people.

We have to attend schools and playdates and extra-curricular activities when we are young. As adults, we have to show up to jobs, go shopping in stores, attend family functions, cultivate friendships, take part in hobbies, and navigate the seemingly endless journey to finding a spouse and raising a family. During all of these situations, we are interacting with others, and whether consciously or sub-consciously, are seeking to make an impression on those around us. Consider this for a moment. No matter where you are going, you take a dedicated amount of time to choose your clothes, prepare your hair and face, perhaps put on accessories. If you are an adult with any manners, you consider what you are going to say before you say it aloud. And depending on where you are and who you are with, you may choose to phrase your words differently or even not say what is really on your mind at all. This is because whether you would like to admit it or not, you want others to view you in a particular way. You may act very kind to others when among your church group, and yet when you are in the supermarket maybe your response to a rude shopper isn't always 'Peace be with you". Personal branding is very much just an extension of what we have been taught to do our entire lives. It is simply a more concentrated and researched effort to ensure that what others think of us is how we *want* them to think of us, and then utilizing that image for personal gain, whether it be financially, socially, or perhaps even both. Doing this does not make someone a sociopath or cold. It is simply recognizing, then using the good things we have to offer to share it with other people. Personal branding is *not* turning a monster into a prince. Rather it is turning a pauper into the prince he could always have been. The majority of people use their personal brand for good, to make people laugh online, sell genuinely innovative products, or endorse their careers to get better opportunities to do what they do best. Isn't that what we all want to do?

The concept of utilizing your personal brand and position to cultivate success was first introduced in 1937 by the author Napoleon Hill in his novel titled *Think and Grow Rich*. Since then, the idea that a person could simply market themselves to see the results and successes they wanted has appeared in countless books and informational guides. This may very well be due to the fact that the media is an essential tool to self-branding, and its use and progression has only increased dramatically over the years. During the 1940s, a person could create a brand only by becoming a prominent figure in society, whether it be an athlete, a politician, a film star, or a radio reporter. These people could quite easily control their personas in the media, as the only means by which people were connected were through radio, print, and small films. Scandals were few. News reports only focused on the important information of the day, so if a rising figure wanted their brand to shine or expand, they could take part in a magazine spread or newspaper interview. Another way that a person could increase their public image was by being asked to endorse a product, and getting placed in radio, billboard, or print ads for the product. When a celebrity endorsed a product during these times, the sales would increase greatly and that celebrity's image would hold strong as being relevant and cool, especially if their product was a new invention or viewed as being risqué.

During the 1950s, 60s, and 70s, the use of personal branding by prominent figures in society only increased with the popularization of television and subsequently television advertising. Politicians could run ad campaigns of themselves holding babies, rescuing animals, and fighting for justice for the people. Celebrities could participate in product advertising and even appear on shows meant to let them show off their personalities and positive qualities, such as game shows, talk shows, or variety shows. People could participate in interviews in media channels that were now far-reaching compared to the media of yesteryears and could reach wider audiences with their brands. Even professionals such as chefs, craftsman, and artists could create programming to not only show people how to create certain things but to also showcase their own unique brand of cooking or painting. Many of these professionals began their own line of supplies so that consumers could more closely mimic their techniques, or at the very least *feel* as if they could. Often, during this time period, those wanting to better increase their public image would publish auto-biographies, cookbooks, or how-to guides. It was also during this time that ordinary people began using personal branding within their own lives to achieve more success.

The 1950s was an era filled with new inventions and products, as well as a time in many ways dedicated to maintaining the traditional ways of American life. A husband was expected to secure a good job that paid well, and a wife was expected to produce lots of children and maintain a clean household. Families were also expected to maintain a host of personal investments, such as new, shiny cars, washing machines, and microwave ovens. Keeping up with the Jones's was no longer a fad, it was a way of life. In order to appear well-off, stable, and modern to all of your friends and neighbors, the average woman was expected to wear the right clothes for her locale, have her hair be styled just so, and have a well-equipped household that was clean and orderly for her husband to come home to. Men were expected to act wholesome and support their families financially by purchasing the best of what was new. Everyone had to ensure they kept their conversations light and pleasant. All of these things were needed to be complete in order for a person to have a rich social life and be viewed with high regard in their communities. When examined, the 1950s cultivated not just the idea of personal branding, but rather an entire culture based around the idea of presenting your best self to others and watching very closely how others regarded you. While during this decade personal branding on a daily basis was focused primarily on being just like everyone else, during the 1960s after the introduction of the counterculture movement, personal branding for most shifted to focusing on what made you unique.

During the 1980s, personal branding techniques became more on point than ever before. For the first time throughout history, self-help books became widely popular as people sought to improve themselves to become more successful. It was during this time, however, that many authors and individuals well-versed in personal success preached the idea that true success came not from self-improvement, but from self-packaging. Everyone has good and bad qualities, and while you can work to improve the negative aspects of your personality, ultimately people will still be people and will still have flaws. However, self-packaging will allow you to present *only* those qualities that are positive and use them to your advantage, creating a more genuine self-brand rather than pretending to be someone or something that you simply are not. The techniques provided by those well-versed in personal branding were utilized by businessmen, entrepreneurs, and professionals alike. It was also during the 1980s that the most important tool for self-branding was invented and marketed; the internet.

When it was first introduced to the public market, the internet was seen by many as a tool for technology geeks and those with less important things to do with their time. Even with the introduction of email, many people still preferred snail-mail to having to log onto a computer and learn a whole new program just to communicate with someone they could easily just call or write. However, as the technology of the internet and personal computers became ever quicker and more user-friendly, the popularization of computer technology for the average person continued to increase throughout the 1980s and 90s, and by the 2000s became a necessity for people to brand themselves personally. In order to be seen as a professional, you had to have a working email, resumes typed using word processing software, and computers that could be used to work on. You could even purchase more and more items online with Amazon or eBay in the 90s, and people could find useful information about you and your career on your website rather than in the phonebook.

The search engine Google was created in 1998, and within just a few years most people shifted to learning things online rather than in books or educational films. Questions could be answered with the push of a button, and similarly, people could find out what they wanted to know about you and your brand in a matter of seconds. 2004 brought the invention of an entirely new avenue for marketing and branding; Facebook. While Facebook was originally intended to be a social networking site to keep you in touch with friends and family, it quickly became a catalyst for people to create entire personas for themselves online. Facebook incited a wave of new media channels, including YouTube in 2005, Instagram in 2011, and Twitter in 2007.

Suddenly, you did not have to be a celebrity or politician or even have a career to have people pay attention to you. If you could create media that people would be interested in, you could become noteworthy. However, these channels quickly became flooded with people from all around the globe who could create interesting videos, posts, and other content for people to view. It quickly became difficult to stand out among the crowds, and this meant fewer opportunities for people to become noticed and for their personal brand to be recognized. This problem was alleviated, however, when content creators for such avenues began to seriously study social media market consumptions and began to focus on cultivating specific branding, marketing it to specific audiences. Once one creator began doing this, it became possible for others to follow suit and create a new portal for people to not only create an online presence but to actually begin to make money off of content. A creator could market a video on YouTube that could garner millions of views, resulting in thousands of dollars of revenue. On revenue free sites such as Facebook, Twitter, and Instagram, a person looking to expand their success opportunities could partner with a product brand and endorse it to make money if they had a large following. They could create their own product lines based off of what content they produced, and even simply sell merchandise with their faces on it. They could even create a personal brand highlighting their knowledge in a particular area of expertise, such as interior decorating, and use it to get a real-life job in the field.

Today, virtually every company has accepted that social media and online platforms are the avenues by which most people receive information and advertisements, and are moving their advertising marketing into those areas. Similarly, personal branding today takes place mostly online, with mainly celebrities or other public figures using other methods such as television or film to reach their audience.

Now that you have a great understanding of what personal branding looks like and how it has evolved until now, we can answer the question of *why* personal branding is important. If you want to be successful *financially*, you have to be able to be a *professional* success. In today's market, there are every day more and more qualified candidates flooding the job market for skilled positions, and even on platforms such as film, television, social media, and online forums, there is an ever-increasing amount of competition and content. The only way in which to stand a chance at securing a well-paying career in any field nowadays is to stand out to employers and audiences alike, providing them with what they want to hear and see. The only way to determine what they want is to *research* what they want and then figure out how to implement it into what you already have going for yourself. Regardless of the specifics of your audience, everyone wants to feel that, if they are paying a person to do a job or taking the time to watch that person, that person is someone unique, someone special, and is providing something that no one else on the market is providing. The only way to do this is to create a very personal, positive brand for yourself and your career, cultivating an image with awesome connotations and selling points.

Those who are unsuccessful at trying to become a musician, actor, YouTuber, a working professional engineer, professor, or even a lawyer is because they did not work on creating a personal brand for themselves. They were content to be just like everyone else, hoping their qualifications and skills would see them through to new opportunities. But there is a fatal flaw in this very common reasoning; ANYONE can match your qualifications. That prestigious university you went to? It didn't say "John Only" under its Latin insignia. The degree you worked for? Anyone with good enough credit for student loans or enough money saved already could have gotten that same degree anywhere in the country thanks to online schools. The skills you worked so hard for were not invented upon your learning them. Countless others had to learn them to achieve the same goals you did. Factor into this equation the very real fact that someone else, always, at any time, will have more experience than you. They may not be looking for the same job as you right now or be living in your area, but someday, they might. And if all you have to hold up to a potential employer or an audience of the world is the same thing they've already seen on someone else's resume or media accounts, you may as well write the phrase "YOU DON'T *NEED ME*" on your forehead. While you should obviously seek to be qualified in your area of career, you need to cultivate that 'je ne sais quoi' personality in order to get ahead and be the one that others look to for more guidance on how they too can become successful.

Ultimately, a personal brand is your best tool for success in 2019. Now that you understand what it is and how it is important, you can begin to work towards cultivating a unique personal brand of your own and take charge of your future!

Chapter Two: An Introduction to Personal Branding in 2019

As you now already know, personal branding in 2019 looks a lot different than personal branding even just twenty years ago. However, the most successful branding techniques from earlier years can still be relevant today; we just have to learn to apply them to newer platforms. In learning how a personal brand can begin successfully and evolve over time to meet the market demands, let us take an in-depth at one of the most influential personal brands of all time: Martha Stewart.

Martha Stewart began her career in 1976 when she created a small catering company with her friend and ran it out of her basement. From there, Martha was hired to manage gourmet food supply stores and continued to grow her catering company. While providing food for a book release party, she was introduced to an influential publisher at the time, who recognized her unique taste and ability to cook and decorate flawlessly. From there, he contracted her to write a cookbook focused on entertaining guests, and in 1982 Martha released her first cookbook entitled *Entertaining*. Within the next 10 years, she would go on to publish more than 10 cookbooks and lifestyle how-to guides, as well as appearing on countless television programs, such as *The Oprah Winfrey Show* and late-night talk shows. She also began writing dozens of articles for newspapers and magazines on homemaking and cooking, and in 1990 developed a lifestyle magazine called *Martha Stewart Living*. From there, Martha went on to create a 30-minute weekly television show in 1993, inviting viewers to create things featured in her magazine, and eventually launched her show to air new 60-minute episodes every day of the week in 1997. During this time she also appeared on *The Today Show* and *The Early Show* and appeared on several different magazine covers.

In 1997, Martha consolidated all of her business ventures under one brand, entitled *Martha Stewart Omnimedia*. She was able to use this company to secure greater ad times for her lines of products, her magazines, and even launched a business website and mail catalog. By 1999, Martha became the first self-made woman billionaire in U.S. history and continues to be one of the richest people in the United States.

Throughout her entire career, Martha has garnered astronomical opportunities for success and wealth. This was not achieved, however, because she was so much better than or talented than anyone else alive at the time. All her successes can be linked to the fact that, from the very beginning of her career, she carefully and meticulously curated a personal brand for her name and persona. She utilized her good qualities, like her knack for home-decorating and cooking and used them to curate a unique style for herself. The pictures featured in her books were elegant and tasteful, but unlike the traditional concepts people were accustomed to. Her decorating styles incorporated themes from New England and yet were universal enough to be used throughout the country, setting her apart from more regional or more general professionals trying to make it in her field. Her recipes were designed to be easy for the home cook to understand, but used fine ingredients and were often meant to impress. Her demeanor was always one of cheer and class, while her wardrobe spoke of simplicity, cleanness, and elegance. She displayed her passion for helping others to entertain and impress by utilizing countless media avenues including print and television to give tutorials and tips for achieving decorations and food like her own. She then very smartly took control of her personal brand even more by consolidating all of her efforts into one company, and aptly gave that company her very own name. She even began a lifestyle magazine, so that others could literally try and achieve a Martha Stewart 'feel' in every aspect of their homemaking. Her personal brand became established as one of the most iconic facets of Americana to date.

Another hallmark of her personal brand was its ability to weather her scandal in 2004. She was charged for insider trading in regards to her company and even spent time in prison. While this greatly contrasted with her 'goody-goody' homemaker image, she launched a re-branding effort in 2005 and actually began another television series that saw wonderful successes, and has continued to publish new cookbooks and lifestyle magazines in the years since. This is mainly due to the fact that, while people struggled to accept her wrong-doing, she *still* provided audiences and consumers with a style and brand that no other could match, because *no one else was Martha Stewart*. While others could have written a similar amount of cookbooks or been on television as much as she was, there was no replacement for her styling, demeanor, and face. Let us take a moment to consider the downfall of another famous cook and homemaker, Paula Dean. While her scandal centered on her use of a racial slur rather than fraudulent gain, one could look at her career and draw many comparisons between her and Martha. They both had successful product lines and were seemingly unique in their presentations. While Martha had a classy, elegant charm, Paula had a humble, down-home drawl. But when Paula's empire fell, there were already several qualified candidates to take her place. The Food network already had other cooks from the south producing shows, and it didn't take long for the shelves of stores like Wal-Mart to clear out their Paula Dean merchandise and replace it with the now beloved Pioneer Woman. However, when Martha was taken off the air, while there were certainly other lifestyle and cooking gurus out there, none could parallel her history and sense of style. At the end of the day, people are more willing to forgive those that they view as irreplaceable or necessary. While I am sure another Martha Stewart-esque icon could emerge in the future, they will not be successful until the original herself steps out of the spotlight.

Martha Stewart Living has continued to reach millions of people by print and has kept up with the times by popularizing various apps associated with the Martha Stewart brand as well as e-letters and website updates. Martha began selling many years ago and to this day continues to sell a wide variety of products associated with cooking, crafting, and home décor, to everything from paper goods to rolling pins to yes, even food and pet supplies. All of her products feature a cohesive color scheme of pastel blue and white, signature colors of elegance and peacefulness. All of her products are available for purchase across her various platforms, and all carry on them her name.

Martha even maintains accounts across social media, using her platforms there to advertise her products and reaffirm her style, by posting pictures of elegant place settings she's created or new ideas she has had for entertaining. She even uses her accounts, such as Twitter, to advertise her partnerships with other companies, offering discounts on their websites with her special codes and telling of how wonderful she believes their products to be. She has even taken plenty of her financial resources and time to participate in a variety of non-profit campaigns and has a special heart for animals, contributing to their rescue and safekeeping. Martha has even created a show with Snoop-Dog to reach a wider audience merely based off of intrigue. *What on earth could a show featuring clean-cut Martha Stewart and street-tough rapper Snoop-Dog possibly be about?* People tune in to answer this very question, and Martha is all the richer because of it. Her various shows from years past are now available on streaming television sites, and her books are available as e-books to keep up with the technological advances of the times.

Ultimately, you can see how Martha's pattern of success lies in her business acumen and ability to curate a unique personal brand for herself and name. Throughout her 40 plus years in the industry, her name has become synonymous with warmth, class, elegance, and entertaining, and this was no accident. She used trigger words for just such things throughout every appearance and book and show she has ever made and has a seemingly endless collection of decorating and cooking segments dedicated to achieving such feelings in your own home. She actively participates in and seeks out paid partnerships with brands that connect to her lifestyle choices. She has utilized, without fail, the most far-reaching and innovative technologies of her day to spread her personal brand to audiences around the country and world. She has identified that while her particular brand will not speak to those in lower-income households or those without a care for interior decorating, she recognizes that *her* audience consists of middle class and upper-class women who want their homes to be pretty and parties to be remarkable. She does not change her ingredient list to cater to what she knows they sell at Wal-Mart and often calls on her followers and viewers to seek out the 'best quality' ingredients or craft supplies. She even makes and sells lines of high-end pet supplies because she is fully aware that members of her audience have money to spare on their pets.

How does her brand survive if it doesn't appeal to most people? It is the sheer fact that while many could not afford her lifestyle, it is the *promise and feelings* a glimpse of her lifestyle create in people. I will never cook a 5-course meal that serves pork tenderloin cutlets in a bolognaise sauce to 25 guests and ends with a line of croquembouches towers. But to watch her create such things makes me feel like someday maybe I could host a fancy party, and THAT is how she appeals to more and more people. And most of all, she does everything she does, all of this, unapologetically. She never claimed to be a woman of the working class family. She never claimed that her recipes would be easy for a working mother to make. All she has ever done is identified her niche market, sold the idea of finer living to even more people to expand her market, and has curated a well put together and elegant image that tells people *'You can trust me'*. Ultimately, Martha Stewart has created one of the most iconic personal brands for herself and has become a multi-billionaire, household name by simply working hard to package herself and everything she has to offer to the media and consumer alike.

Now that you have a firm grasp of what one example of a successful personal brand looks like, we can now begin to explore how personal branding can still lead to success in other areas and career fields. Not every successful personal brand has to become as famous as Martha Stewart or create multibillion-dollar companies and legacies. Average, everyday people can use the same techniques as the most successful and rich people in the world to greatly improve their own lives and cultivate a personal brand for themselves, and understand why doing so is essential to get ahead of the game.

You can even curate a personal brand for yourself for personal reasons. While most people are content to allow their personalities to speak for themselves, often you'll find that the most socially and personally successful people- those with great friends and familial relationships, as well as large followings online- take the time and effort to simply fine tune what they already have going for them. They create well-manicured social accounts that all have a set color scheme and theme. They wear clothing all of a similar style and put on makeup or style their hair regularly. They make the extra effort to control or alleviate their negative qualities and when interacting with others, they ensure they have a good sense of humor and are kind and thoughtful. While this may seem unnecessary to iterate, very few people actually take the time to put a *concentrated effort* into being a good person. Most people tend to think that it will just happen naturally, and if it doesn't, it just wasn't meant to be. However, that notion simply isn't true. We all have good qualities that could make us great people and give us a rewarding social life and reputation if we merely took the time and thought into ensuring we let those qualities and habits shine in our everyday conversations and interactions. Your personal brand is simply YOU, only operating on a clearer frequency and sent in a more palatable package. It lets people know that you care about yourself, and so they should care about you too. Why can't you use the idea of personal branding to implement positive change in every aspect of your life, not just your professional career?

In today's ever increasingly competitive job market, even if you have the skills or education to qualify you for a particular position, employers are now starting to seek out candidates that will not only meet the job expectations but exceed them outside of the workplace. In years past, one could simply print out a resume, set up an interview, and be on the fast track towards securing a coveted position. However, with the use of social media and online marketing techniques skyrocketing in recent years, more employers are choosing to vet applicants online. They will search for your social accounts and see what kind of content you share and follow. They will see if you have any documented experience in the area listed in your profiles on sites such as LinkedIn. They want to see some evidence of your online literacy. While you could have the same or even a superior resume to another applicant, your social accounts could be what sinks you in the running for a position. This is why the idea of personal branding is so important. While Facebook and other sites may have been created with the idea that content would only be shared with people you know in real life, they have now become likened to a dating profile. People understand that the information you provide is supposed highlight your good qualities and beliefs, and these platforms are no longer a place to act comfortably or only put in a half-effort.

Instead, you should take the time to curate each of your accounts to match the best version of yourself that you could be. The internet also has places where you could post blogs or contribute content to organizations that could be associated with your carecr fields, such as marketing, finance, or even sites for teachers, artists, or trades. If you are able to create an online presence, you not only improve your chances at getting a coveted position or advancing in your field, but you also create more leverage and legitimacy for your personal brand to add to your resume and profile. You can also partner with others in your field to establish connections and perhaps provide a potential employer with an informed reference or mentor who could attest to your personal brand and it's worth and value.

Personal branding is also very important even if you are your own boss and hiring officer. Over 85% of available career paths involve some degree of customer service, and consumers want to see a personal brand just as much as potential employers do. If you are able to market your company successfully, that is wonderful. But sooner or later, you will have to increase your edge over competitors. This can be achieved by adding your *personal* brand to your professional one if you haven't already done so. Clients love to know with whom they are doing business and giving money to, and so if you are able to package yourself as a dedicated, passionate professional in your field with unique features a, b, and c, people will choose to come to your business over a competitor. Seeing a smiling face and genuine persona means more than people realize, and while it may seem old-fashioned, it truly is what can set you apart from others in today's marketplace. In the following chapters you will learn the specifics of how to create a personal brand by learning how to achieve the best mindset for the task, creating a custom to-do list, how to define your audience, how to curate your accounts across four different social media platforms, and how to seek out mentors and monitor your progress.

Chapter Three: Having the _**RIGHT**_ Mentality to Build a Personal Brand

Building a personal brand can be a very rough business. It involves a great deal of hard work and dedication, and it can take an extended period of time before you begin to see the results you would like to. This entire process can and will become all the more frustrating if you are not in the right place mentally to undertake it. A personal brand is designed to make you marketable and attractive to consumers, which will mean opening yourself up to the judgment and scorn of the public eye. People who intend to make a profit off of their personal brands online such as Instagram gurus or YouTube stars are constantly bombarded with personal attacks from strangers. You may even be reprimanded by others genuinely trying to help you along in the process, such as by a mentor or consultant. They are there to tell you things that you may not be able to see clearly for yourself and offer an outside opinion. While it is important to remember to stay true to yourself, the input of others is a valuable and crucial resource to the building of your personal brand, and you must be willing to accept constructive feedback as well as be able to ignore hateful comments from those you are not seeking advice from. This is why having the right attitude is important as you begin the process of building your personal brand, and following are some helpful guidelines to implement along the way.

1.) Be positive.

When it comes to building a personal brand, consumers and viewers alike are attracted to positive people. There is no use in trying to become someone or something that you are not, so if you attempt to build a personal brand with only the veneer or appearance of having a positive attitude, then you will be sorely disappointed when you do not yield positive results. There is a lot to be said about social intuition, and many people are able to identify when others are not being genuine. A positive persona makes people feel uplifted, safe, and as if they are able to more easily relate to you personally. Being a positive person means believing in yourself and trusting that you can accomplish the things you set out to. Having a positive mentality and way about you also means that you will be able to find more fulfillment in your work and results.

You may be asking yourself, "Ok, General. So what does having a positive attitude *actually* mean and look like?" Well, while a lot of people are able to try and be positive about the larger, life-changing situations we face, people often forget that the best way to transform positive *thoughts* into *positive attitudes* is the frequency of our positivity. The best way to begin building a positive attitude is to adjust your thought process on a daily basis. No matter what point you are at currently in your life, you can begin by waking up every day and recounting one thing you are thankful for that day. It may be something small, but being thankful is a positive quality that will help you feel better about your situation. Throughout your day when you face problem people or problem situations, you can attempt to find at least one more good aspect than bad. For example, if you have a boss or coworker that is grinding on your last nerve, simply look at them and identify what it is about them that drives you crazy. Ok. They are bossy, disrespectful, and arrogant. Now look at them and find four things you *do* like about them. They are knowledgeable, dedicated, reasonable, and humorous. This may seem to be such a small change, but if every person just took the time to identify the good that exists in this world along with the bad, imagine where we would be right now. At the very least, *you* will be one step further to changing yourself for the better.

Once you have made the effort to try and change your thoughts for the better, you can try extending that positivity towards others. We have all heard the phrase 'fake it until you make it'. That can mean a few different things to people, but the best way I have ever heard it explained is this; if you begin to act like the person you want to be, you will find it easier and easier to behave that way until you actually become that person. Behavior modification is an ongoing process, not an overnight decision. While you may have plenty of positive qualities, none of them will matter until you have the positive attitude needed to bring them to fruition in regards to personal branding. When you have a conversation with others, listen more than you speak. Smile, and try your best to genuinely care about them and what they are going through. When someone comes to you with difficulties, sympathize with their situation and do your best to provide them with a solution and support. Being a positive person in your personal life will make it substantially easier to allow that positive energy to shine through when you go to inject it into your personal branding efforts.

The common consensus is that it takes 30 days to make or break a habit. So make the conviction that having a positive thought process will be the habit you form this month. Have at least two positive interactions with others on a daily basis, and reiterate to yourself the reasons why you want to be a positive person. DO NOT allow those reasons to be money motivated or else you will fail. A good reason would be that having a positive attitude will help you to appreciate your life and success more wholeheartedly. Or perhaps it could be that you want to become more genuinely likable to others. Your reasoning should never be that you want to market your personal brand successfully and this book told you that you needed to have a positive attitude to do so. You absolutely do need a positive attitude to do so. But you need to be able to find your own, personal reason for wanting to have such an attitude in the first place, even if that reason is simply that you know you have good qualities and you don't want to see them wasted because of your negative attitude. A genuine reason you have in your heart is better than a thousand reasons you simply think are the right answer.

2.) Be dedicated.

Building a personal brand is going to take a lot of time and effort. You will need to take many hours to curate your social media pages and then even more hours to keep them up. You will need to invest more time and perhaps even finances into choosing the correct wardrobe and styling for your brand and work to maintain your appearance daily. You will most likely need to put some sleepless nights under your belt in order to create content and even learn new skills if you decide to try and market your personal brand online for profit. All of these things will become overwhelming if you do not have the work ethic and dedication to see them through. One great way to become more dedicated to what you are doing is to make a schedule to incorporate your goals and tasks into your daily routine. Yes, having a schedule will keep you organized and you will be better off in the long run for having done it. But you would be surprised how much easier accomplishing tasks seems and how much more excited you could be when it comes to your work when you have predestined times set aside to work. The to-do list you create won't seem as daunting and you will be far less likely to procrastinate if you feel that you can reasonably accomplish things ahead of time.

Being evicted to building your personal brand also means that you will have to dedicate time and focus to consistency. Your brand will not much of a brand at all if your media accounts, content, resumes, profiles, products, and words don't have a cohesive ascetic and theme. In order to be a unique entity, you must be an entity, not a random hodge-podge of things. This also means ensuring your personal look and appearance remain constant, and your demeanor remains consistent as well. No one looks at Martha

Stewart and says "She's a very well-put-together woman except for those few times she went on Oprah in her pajamas...". It will be easier for you practice consistency with yourself from the start so that when you do begin to experience success, it won't become overwhelming to suddenly feel as if you have to rush to 'keep up' appearances or content. A dedication to your brand and consistency in your work is the firm foundation on which you will build your empire.

3.) Be passionate.

You are going to be trying to sell the idea of YOU. And no one will want to buy what you are selling if they do not believe you are truly passionate about whatever it is you are doing. Having a passion for your work, even if that work is simply self-branding on social media, will be the fuel behind the fire of how dedicated you are in the long run. If you are not passionate about your work, it will be substantially harder to find the motivation to put the effort into working hard and making the time to curate your personal brand. Some say that when you are truly passionate about what you do, you never work a day in your life. However, even those that love the work that they do still feel as if they are working some days. Every effort a person sets out to pursue will involve some tasks that they may not enjoy. The more involved you become in your work and the more responsibility you take on in your branding efforts, the more of those kinds of tasks you will have to take on. They may become monotonous or overwhelming, even leading you to quit your efforts, if you do not have the areas you are truly passionate about to look forward to. A strong passion will lead you through the more difficult or seemingly never-ending trials you will have to face on the road to success, and will give you hope and drive to continue forward.

Having the passion for your work and career will also help you to a better home in your skills and knowledge in your field. While some areas may not require a full college degree in order to be knowledgeable or well trained, every single career path requires some amount of study and know how in order to improve and move on to better opportunities. While on the job training is bound to happen as most people learn best when in the thick of their work, many opportunities will greatly benefit from taking the extra step and making the time to learn more about your field and career through research outside of your workday. This could mean reading books or articles published by those who became successful in your area detailing how you too, can find success. You could conduct online research and find valuable information that will help you achieve your goals or fix a common problem you see happening in your profession. Broadening you working knowledge of, well, your work, could even mean working extra hours from home or testing new theories on your own time. Whatever gaining more knowledge in your field looks like to you, if you want to covet better opportunities for yourself and get ahead of your competitors, you will have to gain this knowledge outside of your average workday. It will seem downright impossible to dedicate any of your personal time to learning more about something if you aren't passionate about that something.

4.) Be focused.

There will be many distractions throughout your journey to build a profitable personal brand. These things can include personal issues and goals, familial situations, or perhaps just the obligations involved in maintaining a household and adult life. There will always be bills to pay, mouths to feed, relationships that need your attention. It is important to maintain a balance between your personal life and professional one, as a life solely dedicated to either facet of yourself will ultimately leave you feeling incomplete. However, one of the unique features of marketing a personal brand is that everything you do IS personal, and you need to have a strong sense of yourself in your personal life in order to succeed in your professional marketing of yourself. Accomplishing any goal in life will require a very large amount of focus, however building a personal brand will ultimately require not only focusing on your professional attributes and skills but also focusing on your unique personal contributions and traits and tailoring them to your desired style. Building a successful personal brand will require a near constant observation of and content creation for your various social media accounts, blogs, and channels. You will have to be focused on your appearance and demeanor when presenting yourself to the world and carefully monitor your behavior to achieve the results you desire. Maintaining this degree of focus may at times prove difficult, but is absolutely necessary to remain in control of your personal brand and curate for yourself the persona you wish to market.

5.) Be willing to ask for input.

Your personal brand is meant to be marketed to other people, right? So how exactly will you know what others think or feel about you and your personal brand if you do not prepare yourself to ask them? When you have a specific vision or plan in mind for your image and persona, it can be difficult to humble yourself and ask for the opinions of others. But you must be in a mindset where you are willing to accept and even seek out the input of others in order to succeed. While not every thought or suggestion from an outside source should be implemented in your brand, it is important to recognize that good feedback and help can come from anywhere and anyone. Acknowledging this and subsequently seeking out feedback will require you to be in a strong enough place within yourself so that you are able to stay true to who you are without being so rigid that you become off-putting to others.

To accomplish this balanced mindset, you need to acknowledge a few things. Firstly, you are uniquely talented and what makes you marketable is non-negotiable. Secondly, you also have to remember that other people will always be able to see a flaw, a consequence of action, or even a positive attribute you are unable to see clearly for yourself. Thirdly, you must know your resource in order to be able to correctly judge the value of their input. A random stranger's word may be taken with a stronger grain of salt than that of your experienced mentor, for example. You should also take a moment to not only gauge the qualifications and experience of your resource but also their motives. What would they have to gain or lose by giving you the input they are giving? More often than not you will find a person's only objective is to help you succeed, allowing you to more easily trust the feedback others are giving you rather than jumping on the feeling of being personally attacked or undermined. Being humble and yet astute and grounded enough to accept and implement the opinions and thoughts of others requires walking a very fine line and balance, but can be achieved so long as you begin your process of building a personal brand with the intention to accomplish these things in your personal mindset and behavior towards others.

6.) Be sure of who you are.

While we will discuss later on the in-depth process of remaining true to who you are and why it is so important *during* the building of your brand, it is valuable to keep in mind *before* building a brand as well. When you first come to the decision that you want to build a brand, you may have an idea of what that will look like. Scenes may come to mind of perfectly coordinated social media pages, a large following on digital streaming channels, and perhaps getting to endorse products or appear in print or television. You may even imagine a less public personal brand wherein you have a great and unique reputation with employers and coworkers alike, or even just among friends and family. No matter what your vision for your own personal brand is centered on, I'm sure the most central factor in your equation was *you*. It would be near impossible for someone with no self-esteem or personal value to decide that they and their personalities were worth marketing. Before the process even began, and all you had was thought to build a personal brand and decided to purchase this book, you could see the amazing and unique qualities that made you think "I can do this!".

You had a voice you knew no one else could mimic and a career or persona that could appeal to an audience. This feeling is the key to being successful as a personal brand and is truly the only way to achieve the goals that you will be setting for yourself and working towards. The world, your audience, your friends and family and mentors, will all be telling you which way to lean and what to wear and how to act. Their input is valuable, but at the end of the day, the only one who has to live with the choices you make is you. Being sure of who you are as a person and what you have to offer is the only way to ensure you will be happy and achieved in this line of work and marketing. Being sure of who you are will perhaps also help you to maintain a grounded moral compass and humility throughout the ups and downs of your career. Once you begin seeing some successes, it could be quite easy if not downright human to begin to feel prideful and full of all your glory. I mean, you are a success, so why can't you feel like you're one, right? However, this type of mindset will always seep into how you behave and speak, and especially if your brand is based in media creation or heavily relies on your persona, you can quickly become off-putting and sink your rising ship. No one from any demographic or audience wants to see a jerk who thinks they're 'all that' try and relate to them, and being arrogant is just a short road to nowhere.

Knowing who you are and where you come from can help you keep you grounded amongst the work that you do, and can also be a source of hope for you if your career and brand face turbulent trials. You will be sure to remember that you still have something to offer no matter where you are at in your journey, and that is a comfort too many forget to utilize. Just take a look at the most well-liked public figures in 2019. Jennifer Lawrence is noted as being one of the most humble and humorous actresses today and did not get that reputation by acting better than those around her. Instead, she makes an effort to make jokes and be a warm presence to coworkers and interviewers alike, never taking herself or her fame seriously at all. She makes a clear point to the world that she loves her work, but not only does not seek fame but rather dislikes that aspect of her work. This quality is what makes her all the more likable to fans and companies looking to hire her, and if you employ a similar attitude and mindset you are sure to be much better off in the long run of your efforts. In contrast, you could examine the low likability of other personal brands due to a dissimilar attitude, such as Kanye West. While we won't be discussing his exploits or opinions that have rocked his image, one defining facet of why many dislike him today is that he has no problem talking about his fame and why he is so deserving of it, even deciding on multiple occasions to talk about how amazing he is. While he will always have diehard fans who respect his honesty and even those who dislike him personally may still enjoy his music, he will always be a divisive and controversial brand, turning off many people and ultimately closing the door on opportunities for his career. While money and success may be of no concern to Kanye anymore, YOU still have to consider those things for yourself and your brand. Do you really want to jeopardize everything you worked for so that you can take a public victory lap? People love humble people who seek to uplift others and be a positive presence for all, not just themselves.

7.) Be purposeful in everything you do.

Finally, you must be purposeful in everything that you do. Basically, this just means that you cannot simply make a career-defining decision without ensuring your every action in this move and all others is purposefully set up to help you achieve your goals in your personal brand. Every picture you post, every video you create, every outfit you style, every interview or blog post you participate in. Every book you read, every class you take, they should all be in service to building your personal brand. Nothing will come out of your action if you do not make it a purposeful action. Making decisions based on purpose and drive will help you to make the most of your decisions and time. Essentially, if every action has a purpose, then o action is wasted. Every action is in service to you and your career, and this mindset will help you further convict you towards your ultimate end game. Do you want to become a YouTube star or Instagram guru? Do you want to land life-changing job offers in your field or create a recognizable brand for your persona? These goals will require a lot of hard work along the way, and to make the most out of your work you will need to make decisions and budget your time with purpose. Even small decisions, such as which color of eyeshadow you wear or what kind of lighting you have in your picture will have an impact on your brand. So make these decisions with purpose and you will see the results you are looking for rather than the results circumstance makes for you.

Ultimately, you will need to keep all of these important things in mind when you first begin to build a personal brand, as well as maintain them and integrate them into your mindset throughout the process going forward. Building a personal brand can be grueling and scary and open you up to a lot of things in life, so it is essential and greatly important that you strive to have the right mindset to accomplish the task and find success. You will need to be a positive person and keep positive thought processes going even in the face of difficulty and setback. You will need to ensure you are dedicated to what you are doing and put the time and effort into your work. Passion will be a key factor in whether or not people invite your personal brand into their lives and whether you are happy and fulfilled when working towards your goals. Having a focused mind will help you to better utilize your time and get a clearer picture of what you want to achieve.

Valuing the input of others will assist you in fine-tuning your personal brand to a wider audience and help you to greater capitalize on what you are marketing. Being sure of who you are as a person and what you have to offer the world will ensure you stay grounded and likable throughout the highs and lows of your brand's success and trials. Finally, being purposeful in everything you do will ensure your efforts are utilized as well as they possibly can be and the future and public imaging of your brand stay in *your* control, not the control of circumstance. If you work to implement these key pieces of advice into who you are as a person and how you react during your journey, you will surely see much more goals achieved than you previously would have and it could quite literally be the difference between success and failure for you and your brand at every stage.

Chapter Four: How to Build a Personal Brand

Now that you understand what personal branding is and what kind of mindset you need to have in order to do it, it is finally time to begin working on building the foundation for your personal brand. This foundational work will be what you build upon as time goes on, and will truly make the difference for you and your personal brand in the long run. Building a personal brand is vitally important if you wish to achieve long-term success in a career that is fueled by being in the public eye or is contingent upon having a reputation with others. Basically, personal branding is essential for most professionals, although it is rarely employed, giving *you* the upper hand in the market for deciding to undertake this journey. This chapter will be divided into two separate sections; what you will need to *have* in order to build a personal brand, and what you will need to *do* in order to build a personal brand. First, let us take a look at the checklist for what you will need to have to begin laying your foundation.

Much like building a house, building a personal brand does not happen overnight. Both involve a great deal of preparation work and planning, both mentally, emotionally, physically, and financially. Once you have prepared yourself for the massive undertaking, you then need to gather the materials necessary for the task at hand before pouring the foundation. Imagine the following checklist as your 'shopping list' for building your personal brand.

Personal Brand Shopping List: What do I need to start building my brand?

- Technology

This is quite literally the first material possession you will need to secure before building your personal brand. While not everyone can afford the brand new, top of the line Mac, it is important to understand the value and vital role that technology now plays in personal branding in 2019. Today, no matter what level of personal branding you wish to achieve, from online stardom to simply securing better job offers, some level of your personal branding will have to be conducted online. No matter what type of personal branding you wish to work towards, you must have a smart device, such as cell phone or tablet that you can carry with you throughout the day and on which you can download the latest apps for social networking. This device should also be connected to a data plan so that you can access your accounts without needing to connect to Wi-Fi.

It may even be beneficial to purchase a spate device on which you could conduct branding business and keep another device for personal use. This is mainly due to the problem or proper device storage. Many modern-day devices now have slots for SIM cards, which are basically small micro-discs you insert into your device to store pictures, videos, and apps on. Once these cards are full, however, you must remove them and insert a new card, which means you no longer have access to all of the things you placed on your old card. While you can change them out regularly, this can become frustrating and a hassle to many people. While your personal social media accounts will be used to build your personal brand, many people still use their phones to store pictures they do not intend to post to social media and apps that they simply use for their personal entertainment, such as games or content players. These apps and games combined with your professional ones can take up a great deal of your device's storage and may very well slow down the efficiency of your connections. So if you can afford the investment, you should seriously consider purchasing a separate smart device so you can keep professional pictures, videos, and apps clear from your other content allowing you better focus and utilization of your limited resources. An inexpensive tablet, for example, could be a great tool to use for such a purpose.

However, there are many people that even maintain a separate smartphone, solely due to the fact that it has all of the capabilities of a tablet, but is also capable of calling and texting. This means you can have a separate work line to answer inquiries for your personal brand without compromising your privacy and still being able to separate out your personal from professional content. Many major chain stores now sell pre-paid smartphones for substantially cheaper rates than contract carriers, which means you could, in theory, spend as little as $150 average to set up and $30 average monthly to maintain a separate smartphone, capable of everything your current phone is. This may even be a more affordable option than purchasing an expensive tablet and data plan. However, if this route still sounds more appealing to you, you could try investing in a number adding service. For a small fee, one of many different companies you chose from will connect your cell phone to two separate numbers and will allow you to answer both inconspicuously, without the caller or texter being notified that they are calling only one phone. This will help you to compartmentalize between your work and professional lives without compromising your privacy or purchasing and maintaining another cell phone.

Once you have your mobile devices and data plans set up, you will also need to ensure you have a desktop or laptop computer to conduct essentials on. While mobile devices are essential for social media, laptop or desktop computers are still necessary for many websites and programs to properly function, such as word processors and video editing software. These products by no means have to be top of the line, as even the lower cost options will still work well. However, it is important to remember that this technology is an investment, and the more work you intend to accomplish on this device, the harder it will be as time goes on if your device is of a lesser quality. If your ultimate goal is simply to curate a personal brand to get better job offers or personal enrichment, then your current laptop or desktop will be just fine. However, if your goal is to rely heavily on technologies to become a YouTube star or eventually run an entire multi-faceted company, then higher quality is best.

On that note, what path you wish to take will also determine what extra technology you purchase from here. YouTube stars often purchase professional portable cameras, microphones, and tripods. They also purchase video editing software programs and other things of that nature which we will discuss further in the book. Anyone seeking social media branding typically purchases lighting equipment. Those who wish to curate brands based off of a particular skill or already somewhat successful career will purchase faster processing computers so as to become bloggers or online experts. Even professionals such as chefs utilize technologies in their trades, such instant-read thermometers or subscriptions to food magazines. Basically, while you may not be entrenched in the process of building your personal quite yet, you need to remember to budget and plan for purchasing these extra technologies and understand the value of investing in them.

- Mindset

We discussed earlier the importance of having a positive mindset for undertaking your goal of personal branding, and you now understand why it is so important. That is why you should include it on your list of things to ensure you have before beginning to work towards building your brand. You need to remember to remain positive and dedicated, and while a mindset is not something you can purchase in the store, it is highly valuable none the less.

☐ Knowledge

The know-how for your chosen career field is not something you can simply buy online or get from being able to say you have a degree. However, it is something that will require a great deal of time, and quite possibly money. Let us say for example that you desperately want to be a YouTube star. While you may be able to invest in the technology necessary for that undertaking, you will also have to invest your time and rain power into researching audiences, demographics, and successful techniques that others have used to become successful. You will also have to research how to use video software and technologies, as well as a variety of things when creating content for new topics and subjects. If your goal is to use your personal brand to become a famous chef, you will need to research the science behind cooking and why foods do the things that they do, why certain techniques work and others don't, and what type of problems your fans can expect to run into when recreating your recipes so they can avoid them in the first place. If your goal is to become an expert engineer and uniquely qualified in your field, while a personal brand will help you to become invaluable and set you apart, yes, you will still have to invest in getting a degree. No amount of personal branding can cover up a severe knowledge gap no matter where you are working, and people will eventually see through your branding techniques if there is nothing to substantiate them. Before you begin a personal branding effort, you have to be knowledgeable in your area. Personal branding is about marketing what you already have going for you, not smoke and mirrors techniques to help you gloss over the hard work necessary for success.

- Body

Yes, this is the oddest sounding requirement in the world. Why on earth would you need the right *body* to start building a personal brand? Well, while we would all like to believe that our society is one of love and not judgment, most of us know all too well that that is simply not true. There are certainly people of all shapes and sizes who have built successful brands, however, you simply have to be aware of how your physicality will factor into your brand, and if it does not convey the image you want, then you need to review your options for changing it. THIS DOES NOT MEAN PLASTIC SURGERY! Too often people get bogged down in this idea because the idea of a presenting your real self when you have flaws is somehow more daunting than the idea of embracing those flaws or working to soften them in other ways. In reality, addressing your physical appearance and how it affects your brand is actually quite simple. You merely need to have an adult conversation with yourself and be honest about how your brand may be affected or shaped by all of the different components of your physical appearance, including your hair, makeup, wardrobe, and body type. If you are a larger person and the brand you would like to build is focused on fashion, then you should consider tailoring your clothing choices to brands that cater to people of your size and celebrate body diversity. Research companies that may want to partner with you and open the door for new opportunities. Also, prepare yourself for the trials you may face in the public eye, but remember that knowing who you are and your value is vital to overcoming these hurdles. Your physical shape does not have to change in order to achieve your goals, you just have to be aware of how they will affect your results and plan accordingly.

If your personal brand is unaffected by your physical body shape, as many brands would be, then it is also important to remember the other aspects of your physical appearance and what message they convey to the world about you and your brand. If you wish to build a blog and personal brand around natural dieting and cooking, then your clothing choices could reflect that by employing natural color schemes and fabric patterns. Perhaps you could research bohemian style guides and looks. You could style your hair and makeup very little so as to downplay any artificial connotations associated with things like heavy makeup looks and hair-dos. If you wish to brand yourself as an ambitious entrepreneur, you could curate your look to include nice suits and few but expensive accessories and a clean haircut and shaven face. Even if these steps don't reflect the style you yourself currently have, there is an ideology called 'wear-apy', wherein you wear clothes that will make you feel a certain way. People change their aesthetic all the time, and you are no freak or fraud for doing the same. If you decide your brand would benefit from you wearing a certain style of clothing and you like doing so, then invest in these looks and eventually they will become a part of who you are and who you present yourself to be. Perhaps wearing these new clothes and styling your countenance differently will even help you to feel more successful and comfortable with the new role you are taking on.

It is important to remember, however, that any change you make to your appearance should be in service to your ultimate goal and desired aesthetic, but should absolutely be a natural extension of who you are as a person and what your special qualities reflect. While we touched on the importance of being genuine earlier and will go more in-depth on the subject later on, your appearance should never make you feel uncomfortable or like a costume, unless of course your brand is somehow built around the playing of a character, such as being a cosplay figure or designer. It will seem absolutely fake and fraudulent of you to take on an entirely different persona and look than what you currently have, but if the qualities you are capitalizing on are a genuine part of who you are as a person, then the physical reflection of those qualities should not appear completely out of the ordinary for you to take hold of.

- Social Skills.

If you are an adult who has trouble interacting with others, it is not too late for you to learn how to be sociable. While the vast majority of people have a group of friends, colleagues, or relatives they are most comfortable with and can't talk to easily, many adults today struggle when meeting new people and can feel uncomfortable in heavy social situations. If you are deciding to take on the task of building your own personal brand, however, then you have to be able to overcome your fears and anxieties. While every successful personal brand is different and the positive qualities the person possess vary greatly, the common skill that every personal brand must have is an ability to talk openly and comfortably with others. Not all of us were born with the gift of gab, but everyone can gain it if they are willing to put in the hard work.

Working on your social skills is like pouring fresh chum into shark-infested waters without a lifeboat. Yes, it will seem that scary, because the only way to unlock that door around your mouth and mind is to immerse yourself in difficult social situations and force yourself to talk to other people. Take some time out of each day and find at least two new people to talk with. Approach them first, introduce yourself, and begin talking to them about something relevant. If the conversation goes well, keep it going until you find that one of you has to leave. Do this for two weeks straight, and then work on finding more stressful situations, such as a party or get together. Attend it solo and make a determined effort to talk to every new person you can. The more you talk with a person the more comfortable you become with them, so while it will feel excruciating and awkward, find another new person to talk to after a short time. When you build a personal brand, you have to learn how to be consistent in the delivery of your personality and dialect, no matter what situation you are in or with whom you are speaking. This means you have to behave the same way in your videos, pictures, interviews, and daily conversations.

Even if your lone purpose in personal branding is to secure better job opportunity, you will have to be consistent when talking with one potential employer to the next and maintain that demeanor and report once you start working. This is yet another reason why it is so important for you to be yourself; you cannot be a fake person every day for the rest of your career. You may as well be yourself from day one. Developing your social skills may take a long period of time before you finally feel one hundred percent comfortable with every situation, but so long as you begin actively working on improving them before you begin setting up your personal brand, you should be able to interact with others well as needed during the process of pouring your foundation. You will know you have succeeded when you can talk with others easily in most any situation. You will hopefully begin to realize that, just as you found you had small things in common with strangers, you will certainly have something in common with virtually anyone you meet.

Now you have the technology you will need to set up the foundation of your personal brand, as well as the knowledge, mindset, and physicality to lay the groundwork for your goals. When you have developed social skills, you are able to talk with people off from all walks of life and appeal to a wider audience. This means you can now begin the process of actually setting up your brand and getting just that much closer to establishing yourself as a force to be reckoned with in the marketplace and find the success you deserve.

Step by Step Guide for Beginning to Build Your Personal Brand

1.) Identify what you have to offer and where your value will lie.

We all have qualities that make us unique, and each of us has a special something that makes others want to get to know us. Perhaps you have a winning smile or a great sense of humor. Maybe you're able to see things that others can't and give great advice on the subject. These positive aspects of your personality will be the things you will focus on going forward in the process of your personal brand. After all, personal branding has been described as selling the idea of a relationship with you to other people. So sell them the best experience possible. If you are having trouble identifying your best qualities, it would be a perfect opportunity to begin to enlist the help of those who know you best. Ask your friends and family what it is about you that they enjoy most. Take a sampling of several different people to ensure that the results of your test are not biased or hyperbolic due to one person's input. While your entire list should not be comprised solely of what others tell you, getting to hear what other people see in you may help to act as a catalyst for your own discovery of what you like about yourself. This is not the time to focus on your flaws and how to improve them. Rather this is the time to focus on the things that are great about your personality and work to increase them and package them as an essential, irrevocable part of who you are.

Your good qualities do not have to only be things about your personality. You could incorporate many good things about yourself from different areas of your life. Everything has some value in what you bring to the table when you decide to pursue a personal brand for yourself. For example, you could have a great knack for wardrobe styling and color coordination. Perhaps you could have a superior knack for tech or programming. These are what I like to call 'ancillary attributes'. They are not the main personality traits that you will be packaging in your personal brand and marketing, nor are they the *main* skill, career, or trade that you will be capitalizing on. They are smaller, less pronounced but still significant skills that you have that may very well help you along the way. Even if you decide your main endeavor is to become an acclaimed cookbook author, having a great sense of technology could help you to explore new and innovative avenues to deliver recipes and create content for food lovers around the globe. If you are talented with color schemes and décor but your primary goal is to be a YouTube vlogger, perhaps you could create some videos based around your work in interior design and even write blogs or articles on the subject. Basically, the best kind of success stories is of renaissance personas, i.e. people who do lots of things well instead of only one thing very well.

Once you have determined your positive personality traits and your ancillary skillset, it is now time to find your primary selling point.

Perhaps you have a skill with cooking, fashion, music, design, art, or comedy. Perhaps you are passionate about a specific cause or lifestyle. Maybe your main selling point is simply a package of all the things that make you relatable and interesting. Whatever this primary skill is, even if it is simply your personality, you can absolutely use it to create an influential and remarkable personal brand. It may require a great amount thought in order to narrow down your list of traits and skills, as people can have many interests but should primarily focus on one main venture, especially when first starting their personal brand. You want to become a renaissance persona, but not to pursue so many avenues at the same time that none of them can succeed.

Kim Kardashian was simply famous for being *Kim Kardashian* for years before she actually did something, capitalizing solely off her name and brand persona. Martha Stewart did not begin television shows, websites, apps, and magazines at the same time she began her cookbooks. She started with what she knew best and understood what her main objective was. Martha then built upon that foundation of success to build an even better and stronger personal brand, always ensuring to incorporate what she was known best for, her cooking and décor skills, into every new venture she pursued. An eclectic brand foundation is a weak brand foundation, and will not be strong enough to hold up the house you build upon it. You will always be able to use the best of what you have to offer, just perhaps not in a primary way initially. If you have a lot of great or positive qualities and skills, you could come up with several possibilities for your primary selling point, however, during the next steps in the process you MUST narrow it down to one. Below is a possible example of what your qualities list could look like.

Personality Traits

- *Funny, mom said I am always making her laugh with jokes. A coworker said that I crack him up at our lunch break. A sense of humor is sarcastic, observational. Tend to poke fun at others without hurting feelings or going too far. Spouse says I make the most jokes about myself when in private.*

- *Informed, always researching current events and both sides of political arguments, can repeat that information back to others and am passionate about doing so, can process information and incorporate historical, cultural, and economic significance*

- *Creative, best friend says I am always seeing things differently and in multiple ways than others, I like to see things and get the full picture, leave no stone unturned, and get excited about any kind of new project*

Ancillary Skills

- *Public Speaking, am always comfortable speaking with others and can talk on a stage, in front of friends, or even enemies with ease and respect, can make up what I'm going to say on the fly or enjoy writing things down ahead of time*

- *Crafting, building things, am always working on a new project, focus on wood and metal mediums*

- *Technology, brother says I am pretty constantly looking into new tech devices and plans for where technology is leading the future, keep myself up to date on newest inventions and products and theories yet to be realized*

Primary Selling Point possibilities...

- *Teaching, creating videos, books, blogs, etc about current vents or history?*
- *Talking, podcasts, interviews, public voice?*
- *Creating, using crafts, selling on platforms, could somehow incorporate current events?...*

Once you have your profile of qualities, it will be time to move onto step number two, which is researching your different options for personal branding.

2.) Research different types of personal brands and decide on one for yourself.

As we have mentioned before in this book, there are different levels and types of personal branding, and each is ideal for a particular set of goals you would like to achieve. The most simple and common form of personal branding is inter-personal branding, wherein you curate a persona and social accounts for the people in your personal life, such as friends and family. While this initial thought may seem deceptive or sociopathic, it really is just a slightly more concentrated effort to do what we have all been taught to do since day one of our existence here on Earth. We do not say certain things to others because of how it may make us look, we do not flaunt or open up about our flaws until we get to know others well. Essentially, inter-personal branding is just taking our natural tendencies one step further and giving our social lives more attention. This could involve fine-tuning and polishing your social media accounts to have a cohesive theme and professional aesthetic. You could quite easily tailor your personal style to be a bit more cohesive if it isn't already. You would most likely decide to be slightly more reserved than perhaps you used to be or others you know currently are, choosing to only present the best of your positive traits when initially meeting or talking with other people. After reading what inter-personal branding looks like, you may have just now realized you have been doing this all along, as have many people you know and love. It is such a common practice some people may even be totally oblivious to its existence. The practice of inter-personal branding will, however, be essential when moving on to more intense styles of personal branding in 2019.

The next level of personal branding is professional personal branding. Essentially, this type of branding is for when a person wishes to simply take their professional skill set and self-package it with their professional skills in order to appeal more desirable to potential or current employers. When creating this type of personal brand, one would simply add more profession-related content to their already curated personal social media accounts, such as posting articles related to work subject matter and posting pictures of themselves in more professional settings, giving their audience the impression that they are passionate about and dedicated to their work. A person seeking to cultivate their professional personal branding would also seek to highlight their personal attributes well, the same way they would have at level one. Some even decide to take it a step further and seek out opportunities to publish information or create content related to their field, so that when interviewing with or submitting resumes to potential employers, they can provide them with links to their various contributions and appear more educated and relevant in the area of work. Most using professional personal branding would also decide to create profiles for professional networking sites, such as LinkedIn. This type of branding is ideal for any working professional today, as it will absolutely help anyone to achieve greater employability and pay rates. As we discussed earlier in the book when addressing why personal branding is so important, we were reminded that *anyone* can match your qualifications, experience, and skillset. People you are competing with for a job may even have similar personal attributes. What will set you apart from the completion, however, is which of you puts forth more effort in presenting your career and self as the best possible option for the task at hand. While you already know and understand how important personal branding is in 2019, many people are still unaware of how personal branding techniques will help them flourish, so the odds are very much in your favor that you could perhaps be one of the only candidates in any job you apply for that is actively curating themselves and their careers for professional advancement.

The highest level of personal branding is, well, just called personal branding. It is what most people think of when they think about what personal branding is, as the lower two levels are essentially only partially utilizing personal branding techniques. Personal branding in its fullest form is when you package your personality, face, name, aesthetic, social accounts, and skill set to market to the broader public eye. This type of personal branding requires the most effort and work, but can also quite often reap the most reward. Many people who set out to turn their lives in recognized brands find some degree of recognition in the public eye and success either online or in other media outlets. Those who chose this type of personal branding often have to create content that is very innovative, creative, and entertaining as the markets for things such as books, movies, YouTube videos, and social media content are currently overflowing with new creators every day. The purpose of personal branding is to set yourself apart from these other creators and be able to cultivate a following that will supply enough revenue to live off of, and once you begin to experience some successes will hopefully be enough to fund the launching of new streams of revenue and ventures. If you are having difficulty picturing examples of personal branding based careers, there are plenty of notable examples all around you. We have already mentioned Martha Stewart and her ability to go from cook to billionaire. Kim Kardashian simply used her aesthetic, name, and personality to create a brand so popular she has now delved into makeup, fashions, and modeling. Even many notable YouTube creators such as Shane Dawson, Jeffree Starr, and Simply Nailogical have become household names from creating online videos and have begun their own product lines in their respective areas of clothing and makeup.

Now that you have an understanding of the three different levels of personal branding, you need to examine your current lifestyle and what you want your future to look like. While a lot of people may say that full-on personal branding is clearly the best option for your life, only you will have to live with the decision you make the subsequent outcomes. Take the time to sit down and examine your familial and social obligations. Do you have a spouse and children that will need your financial and time-related support? Do you have an active and rich social life that really only working a normal 9-5 job will help you to maintain? Where do you want to be 5 years from now? How about 10 years from now? At the end of the day, only one of these options will best suit the life you want to live and the needs of those involved in your life. During this time you will also to have to be realistic about what you can and cannot achieve. Through personal branding, anyone can become more noteworthy and achieve much greater success than they would have before. Many, many skills and attributes are translatable into creation mediums, even if you may initially not believe them to be applicable to the fullest level of personal branding. However, you also have to take into consideration the market saturation of whatever it is you are wanting to market your personal brand is. It will be more difficult to become a YouTube beauty guru in 2019 than it was even five years ago. You have to be able to recognize your strengths and come up with creative ways you can utilize them to fulfill the level of branding that you desire. Personal branding is not a guarantee of success, but rather a tool you use that is guaranteed to *help* you succeed if you put in the time and work.

3.) Set goals.

When delving into a new personal branding venture, no matter what level you aspire to compete, you need to set goals for yourself so that you can feel a sense of accomplishment to keep you motivated, stay focused on the task at hand, and be able to track your ongoing progress. Setting goals will help you stay focused. This is because you will have a set list, right in front of your very eyes, that will remind you of all of the things you have yet to overcome but will also help those things seem less daunting. I mean, if they can fit on a piece of paper or board, they can't be that scary, can they? They also help you to feel a sense of accomplishment because you are able to cross things off as you go and be reassured that you have not wasted your time or talent. This is also how you are going to be able to gauge your ongoing progress and be able to prove to yourself and to others that your hard work was worth it. Setting goals will also help you to gauge what is and is not realistic in your journey and will help you to more clearly see the outcome of all of your hard work. Goals can either be big or small, so long as they are specific, timed, and realistically achievable with the time and resources allotted to them. Setting goals will be like having your own personal checklist of the major hurdles you are going to overcome, and it can be very helpful to understand everything that it left for you to accomplish, as well as serve as a pleasant reminder of all of the things you've already accomplished.

Setting goals is not making a checklist for your life plan. Rather, it is the checklist you make so that you can *create* a life plan. It helps you to keep a 'big-picture' perspective, even when things seem most difficult. Every person's goals will be different but goals, in general, tend to land in one of the different categories. Personal goals are goals that you set to accomplish within your personal life, such as how you interact with family or setting a number of new friends to make. When it comes to personal branding goals, people can set their eyes on many accomplishments depending on what level of branding you are going for. If you want to make a professional brand, you could set a goal that you will create 3 new blog posts or articles in the next month relating to your field. If you are seeking a full-forced personal brand, you could set period goals for reaching numbers of followers to your social accounts or views to your videos or publishers to send your book. In order to get a good sense of what setting goals really looks like, let us take a look at our example profile from earlier.

Name: John Smith, age 30

Personality Traits

- *Funny, mom said I am always making her laugh with jokes. A coworker said that I crack him up at our lunch break. A sense of humor is sarcastic, observational. Tend to poke fun at others without hurting feelings or going too far. Spouse says I make the most jokes about myself when in private.*

- *Informed, always researching current events and both sides of political arguments, can repeat that information back to others and am passionate about doing so, can process information and incorporate historical, cultural, and economic significance*

- *Creative, best friend says I am always seeing things differently and in multiple ways than others, I like to see things and get the full picture, leave no stone unturned, and get excited about any kind of new project*

Ancillary Skills

- *Public Speaking, am always comfortable speaking with others and can talk on a stage, in front of friends, or even enemies with ease and respect, can make up what I'm going to say on the fly or enjoy writing things down ahead of time*

- *Crafting, building things, am always working on a new project, focus on wood and metal mediums*

- *Technology, brother says I am pretty constantly looking into new tech devices and plans for where technology is leading the future, keep myself up to date on newest inventions and products and theories yet to be realized*

Primary Selling Point possibilities...

- *Teaching, creating videos, books, blogs, etc... about current events or history?*

- *Talking, podcasts, interviews, public voice?*

- *Creating, using crafts, selling on platforms, could somehow incorporate current events?*

Type of personal branding creating*: full-level. Want to create a YouTube channel where I make artwork based off of current events and topics affecting our society, maybe some historical pieces as well. Will also use social media and website to market and sell my artwork.*

As you can see here, John has decided to seek a full-level personal brand due to his qualifications. He had a knowledge and skill set that he could use to create content online and artwork in real life that very few people had seen before. He does have a spouse who is able to support them financially while he establishes his presence and works on his videos. He does not have experience making or editing content but is confident he could learn due to his love for tech. He is beginning to think about where this career could take him and is starting to set goals. He understands that further on in the process of creating his personal brand these goals may fluctuate or change, but he feels he needs a clearer picture and timeline of what exactly he is going to be working towards.

Goals in the next month...

- *Make Twitter, Instagram, Facebook, and YouTube accounts geared towards my artwork and current events*

- *Decide on a physical look for myself and brand*

- *Set up a website to begin selling my pieces of work*

- *Install video software and learn how to create intriguing videos*

- *Publish adds across social sites to attract followers*

- *Publish my first video*

- *Start a hashtag for my work #johntheartistspeaks, #johnsmiththinks, etc...*

Goals in the next six months...

- *Continue making a new video and piece of work every week*

- *Reach out to other YouTube creators who focus on political issues, current events, history and introduce them to my work and see about a collaboration*

- *Reach out to podcasts that focus on artists and or news and see about a collaboration*

- *Reach out to other social media influencers to see if they would be interested in collaborations or following my work*

- *Publish adds across social sites to get more followers*
- *Set up a blog and or website that takes an in-depth look at the issue or historical piece I am focusing on each week*
- *Submit my portfolio of work to be nominated for awards that I could qualify for and notify media reporting outlets of my work and nominations*

Goals in the next year...

- *Reach out to publishers, submitting pictures of my work and see about publishing a book of photos from my work and behind the scenes*
- *Try and book an appearance or interview on television or online media*
- *Get involved in activism and find a cause to create a series of work based on*
- *Reach out to companies that make tools and products I use for sponsorship for my*

> *videos and perhaps a marketing deal for their products*

- *Have my Facebook followers, YouTube subscribers, twitter followers, and Instagram followers all exceed 100,000*

- *Create merchandise featuring pictures of his artwork and quotes*

As you can see, while all of the details of his plan are not firmly cemented, he now has a clear picture of where he wants his career to take him. You too can create a clear vision for yourself and your personal brand by creating a list of goals similar to the one John made, only catered to your specific wants and needs. Do not be afraid to change this list as certain possibilities become better opportunities and other opportunities fade off or become irrelevant. If you still need guidance as to what you realistically can and cannot achieve, try researching examples of people whom you admire. Then go on to take a very in-depth look at their career and how they were able to get to the place you want to be. What resources did they have that you do? Which resources did they have that you could get? What was it that attracted people to them in the first place? What was different about what they were doing that landed them in the place they are in right now?

4.) Identify your audience.

We will be discussing how to define your audience more in-depth at a later point in the book, however, it is the next step you will need to do when starting your own personal brand. If you are seeking to create and inter-personal brand, then your audience would be friends and family. If you wish to cultivate a professional-brand then your audience is potential employers or current employers in your field. When seeking to create a new and full personal brand for yourself, then defining your audience becomes a bit more complex. You have to conduct some market research and find out what people, living in what areas, and from which age group and economic statues your content and brand would most appeal to. These categories could range anywhere from teenage girls on the west coast to middle-aged housewives in New England. While there is no formula for personal taste, demographic and market research data exists for a reason; so that people who want to market what they are selling to others can use their limited resources more efficiently. When running an ad on Facebook, for example, you do not want to pay money so that it is sent to people who would have no interest in what you are doing.

Let us again look at our example of John Smith. He is currently working on setting up a personal brand focused on combining art, news, history, and content creation to bring things to the attention of the public and sell his real-life work. His videos are styled with drama and dark color schemes, only allowing light to illuminate his works and the hands that create it. Over a lapsed period of time you begin to see the world he creates take shape, and listen to poetic and sadly sweet music. He includes links in his descriptions so that you can earn more about his work or the event he brings to life. While many people are bound to find this interesting, market research suggests that his target audience is not, in fact, teenage girls or teenagers in general. His work is also less likely to be sold or watched in places such as the South East as many of the events he chooses might be perceived as pro-liberal or anti-conservative. Elderly folk is also less likely to enjoy what he is doing as it is an abstract interpretation and less popular than the art and content they are used to. Research also suggests that people over the age of 65 are less likely to have accounts or be as active with their accounts anyway. So when he goes to publish ads or market his work, he chooses to select men and women from age 20-50, living in the Pacific Northwest, Southwest, and New England regions. He also uses keywords to refine their interests such as art, news, current events, politics, and crafts. This ensures that his advertisements go to people who will actually be likely to watch his content and buy his products when they see his ad.

Market research and knowing his audience will also help John to not change what he does in order to cater to people outside of his target demographic. Just as we discussed earlier, Martha Stewart does not use canned cranberry sauce because she knows her audience would rather make it from scratch because yes, they have the time and the money. If people want quick and affordable recipes they can make they can watch Sara's Weeknight Meals. Defining your audience helps you to remain focused and better target those who will contribute to your profits.

5.) Find your team.

No one can create a personal brand alone. You will need a team of people to help support you and guide you through this process. Those who help you emotionally could include anyone from friends or family. These people could even help you gain resources and can invest financially or with their time in helping you to launch your brand. You will need people to be there for you when the trials come and you feel like giving up. Let the people closest to you know how important it is to you that you make it in this career field and that your brand succeeds. If they are truly there for you unconditionally they should be your cheerleader no matter what. Those who could be your support system on a purely professional level would include people such as coworkers, colleagues, and mentors. We will discuss the importance of mentors later on in the book, but for now, you should understand that mentors are essentially people who have been where you are and can help you to navigate the things they had to learn for themselves or from their mentors. Coworkers and colleagues will help you by being a listening ear that will understand what you are going through, and you will each have something you can offer each other. This could be solid advice, new tricks or techniques they just discovered, or even collaborations for videos or projects. Your team will the rock on which you build and support your house, and you'll need them to be there for you, even if at times you just simply need to know that someone *is* there for you.

6.) Identify and gather your resources.

Resources are essentially anything that you can use to further your brand and accomplish your goals. The common school of thought is that there are three types of resources; time, talent, and treasure. Your time is any tie that you and your team members invest in building your personal brand. In order to evaluate what kind of time investment you can make, you must look at your current lifestyle and the availability of your team members. If you work a 9-5 job and do not intend on giving it up when launching your personal brand, you have to understand that you will have to invest more talent and treasure into your venture to make up for that deficit. In regard to talent, you have already taken stock of this resource before beginning this process.

Factor it into your profile as a reminder of what you have going for you.

Finally, when you evaluate your treasure, this can include money as well as material possessions. Things such as the technology you've already invested in, the software you have purchased, your new wardrobe, they all contribute to the amount of treasure you have to contribute to your personal brand. Investing your material wealth, however, involves a greater risk than your time or talent, as if you fail in your new branding efforts because you did not put in the work, you can still walk away with your talent and while your time is gone, you are given new time every day. Your wealth is the only investment you cannot recover, so you must be sure to take the time to examine what wealth you are willing to sacrifice to things such as video investments, product lines, or advertisements. To get a better picture, let us take a look at what John found when taking stock of his personal investments.

Time...

- *Left my day job,*
- *Family obligations and household duties take up several hours a day*
- *Overall, have about 12 hours a day to contribute*
- *My spouse is willing to help me set up accounts, check their progress, and even contact collaboration partners for me*
- *Colleagues have offered to help me spread the word about my channels and work*

Talent...

- *Skilled craftsman*
- *Creative*
- *Thoughtful*
- *Enjoy teaching others about the world and politics*

Treasure...

- *My spouse is able to pay the monthly expenses for several months until I start seeing revenue*

- *I already own a cell phone and have purchased another. My laptop is now equipped to edit videos, and I have purchased studio lighting, voice recording equipment*

- *Have affordable art supplies and a supplier to get more when needed*

- *Have a new wardrobe that appears artsy but serious*

- *Have a nest egg to invest in ads and opportunities*

You may look at John's list of resources and realize you can't quite match all of his blessings. However every person has been given some things that they could invest into a personal branding effort, and you just have to examine where your resources are and gather them together to truly ensure that your personal brand is going to be an available option for you at the moment. There is no shame in acknowledging that you may have to put your goals off for a period of time while you save money and other treasures to invest in your personal brand, or perhaps you may have to wait until you reach a point in your life that you can invest more time and energy into your reaching your goals. So long as you understand that personal branding is your best option for your future, the techniques will still be waiting here for you to implement further down the road. It is worthy to note, however, that the market for your particular persona and talent may not still be vacant in the future, as if there is a gap in the market, there is always someone eager to fill it. Remember this and try to do your best to accomplish your goals sooner rather than later.

7.) Make a schedule.

Yes, your parents and teachers were right all throughout grade school; you need to budget your time! Your time is clearly a valuable resource, and unlike when we were younger, our time as adults is much more limited. We have houses to clean, kids to feed and drive pretty much everywhere, spouses to woo and jobs to go to. Your time will almost always slip away from you unless you make a concentrated effort to plan your days and nights ahead of time, and, this is the most important part, STICK TO YOUR SCHEDULE. You have wasted even more of your time if you have made a schedule and not stuck to it. At this point, you have hopefully had an honest review of your lifestyle and what type of personal branding you can realistically achieve in accordance with your other priorities, and also have some idea of the amount of time you can invest in your endeavors. This is the perfect time to buy a planner with sets spaces for days, weeks, and months so that you can take just 30 minutes at the beginning of each week to help you better budget your time. Sit next to your family calendar and fill in all of those plans and obligations first, followed by social calls and house maintenance. You may not enjoy this next part, but at this point, you may have to consider cutting certain things if you are unable to find sufficient amounts of time to build your personal brand. See which friend you could push until the weekend or the date night you could reschedule. Every life needs balance, and those closest to you will understand that you are trying to build a better life for yourself and the ones you love.

8.) Begin pouring your foundation.

At this point, you have identified what you have to offer the world. You know which type of personal branding you want to pursue and have set goals for your new career that is just brimming with possibilities. You have identified your target audience and have the best team possible on your side. You have a gathering of resources to use as needed, and a schedule to help you stay on track. It is finally time to begin the tangible work of creating your personal brand. This means finally changing your social media accounts (more information on that found in chapters 7-11), dressing in your new wardrobe, and creating content for your audience. This could mean making videos, posting pictures, or simply making informed articles and blog posts. You can also revamp your resume to include your new ventures and go out of your way to find new opportunities to invest your time into and places to market your personal brand. Whether it be a craft, trade skill, or simply persona that you are packaging along with your name and personality, it is time for the world to get to experience everything that you have to offer. Keep this step by step guide as a reference so that you can continue to come back to it as needed.

Chapter Five: The Importance of Being Yourself

The basis and foundation of your entire personal brand is *you*. People expect you to be unique but also to be relatable. This is why it's so important that you not only be yourself but be the *best* *v*ersion of yourself that you can be. When marketing and self-packaging your own unique style, consumers, employers, and people in your personal life alike are able to tell when the behavior that you give them is genuine or fake. One of the most important qualities human beings can have and one of the best qualities that people tend to look for is honesty and realness. People will not buy what you were selling if they don't believe it is real and comes from a genuine place inside yourself. Over the course of history, many misguided entrepreneurs have believed that lying or deception are good ways to sell products. While unfortunately sometimes these people do see success, this kind of mindset is detrimental to the idea of personal branding. This is because unlike products, your personal brand cannot simply be redesigned or repackaged and resold by a different company. Your personal brand is you, your name and your face, all of which are vitally important to your overall personal brand and cannot be changed.

One thing the average person absolutely loves to hear is it the celebrity, icon, or professional that they see on TV, print media, or on social media is really just the same in real life as they are in the media that they present to others. One of the most disheartening things people can find out is that their hero, or that a personal brand that they love to follow, is truly unlike what they are presenting to the world. This kind of revelation can even be fatal to a personal brand, especially if most of your personal brand is not based on a talent or skill but rather the attributes and personality that you present to others. As we discussed earlier, Martha Stewart was able to become the largely successful mogul that she is today because of her overall unique style and pleasant presentation. On that same note, she became irreplaceable in her field and thus had a stronger personal brand that could survive the hurdles that all people who market themselves as brands may eventually face.

This is another reason why it is so important to be not only yourself but *uniquely* yourself. While we were all raised to believe that we were each a unique little snowflake, in the adult world it may be a lot harder than we realized to differentiate ourselves from others. When building a personal brand, it is essential that you identify what separates you from the rest of the crowd especially if you are pursuing a career in media content creation or are one of many people with your particular set of skills and talent. This is why the top entrepreneurs who have successfully marketed personal brands recommend that before starting your personal brand, you take the time to sit down and evaluate your own special personality traits and those things about yourself that attract others to you. This can be done in a variety of ways but many believe the best way to do this is 2 take just a few hours and have an honest conversation with yourself about your life thus far. Take this time to try and identify patterns that you've seen all the way from early childhood until now. Are you someone who frequently goes out of your way to help others? Do you often serve as a listening and caring ear to others? Are you able to converse with other people in a comfortable and energetic manner? Or maybe are you able to debate others and get your information across with conviction and passion? What words best describe you? Are you smart, funny, kind, or caring? Are you dedicated to your job or are you highly passionate about a certain field or area? These are all things that you can use to market your personality and or skill in the best way possible.

After you've been able to identify several key positive traits that you believe other people would like to see from you that you already possess, it is a very good idea to now approach those who know you best in your life and get their opinions. Ask them what three words would best describe you, and if those words do not match up with your own list or your own idea of what you believe your personal brand should reflect then perhaps ask them what you could be doing better to achieve different results. Ask other people, such as friends, family, co-workers or other people you socialize with regularly what kind of behavior patterns they see from you. Do they see that you're always taking a moment to help out your friends even when it means less time to do things for yourself? Or maybe do they see that you tend to be quick to anger and have a bit of a short temper that you could improve upon before trying to Market yourself as a whole?

Ultimately, when you were creating and building a personal brand, your ultimate goal is to sell that brand to others. These quote on quote 'others' would include people just like your friends just like your family just like your co-workers and just like the other people you socialize with. So no matter how close they are to the situation or how much you believe you need to take their opinion with a grain of salt, you have to come to accept and even celebrate the fact that their opinions will very much help you along this journey. When building a personal brand or even maintaining one, there is a definite propensity by many people to try and take on qualities that aren't true of themselves. Let us say for example that one quality you really admire but don't really have yourself is a selfless spirit It's not that you're selfish per say, it's just that you don't tend to find it easy to always be considering the opinions of others before you consider the opinions or needs of yourself. While trying to be a decent human being, in general, is always a good thing, trying to build your entire brand around the idea that you are selfless is just a recipe for disaster. It may be a quality that you want and that someday you may have, however, if you do not possess that quality a great deal right now, then it would be false to try and market your brand and your persona as having that quality. We all have areas in which we thrive in areas in which we can just survive. There is no shame in admitting that you have shortcomings and rather than focusing on your shortcomings, you should take the time to focus on your positive qualities and what makes you great. Once you've identified these areas, then your focus should be on amplifying those behaviors.

Being honest also entails ensuring that the skills, experience, and ideas you claim to possess are in fact true. We have all been guilty of padding or embellishing the truth now and again. Regardless of the moral implications of doing this, the professional repercussions will be severe. When you are under scorn or judgment from a potential employer or the public eye, things done in the dark will always come to light. People will find out that you only spent 1 year at La Cordon Blue instead of 2. Someone will know that the work order you got wasn't really from a top-paying client, but rather from your parent's friends. If you are willing to stand in your truth and market yourself as you are, then people will be willing to accept that you are not perfect. If your positive qualities are good enough and the content you create entertaining enough, often people do not even care about your experience or income or status in your field. Just take a moment to remember all of the people who simply got their start in careers on social media. They did not attend Harvard business school and yet they may now be more successful than someone who did. Even Instagram accounts for dogs get more followers than accountants, because I mean, of course, why wouldn't they? Take some comfort in knowing that even if you fail at starting a personal brand due to some unforeseen factor, you have a second chance so long as you have a corgi. Be honest about yourself and who you are, and there will still be an audience that wants to buy what you are selling.

Chapter Six: Defining Your Audience

As we discussed earlier, defining your audience is essential to creating your own personal brand. It is the process of examining your body of work and what you have to offer, followed by an intense dive into market research and what it tells you about how well or poorly you and your content will sell among different demographics. Defining your audience also entails conducting your own personal research as well as introducing common sense into the equation. You do not have to pay a market research analyst money to figure out that your fashion blog geared towards LGBTQIA youth is not going to circulate well in the over 65 communities of Boca Raton, Florida. While every person is an individual and it can seem cold or even heartless and sociopathic to boil people down to demographics and age ranges and taste, but at the end of the day it is not going to be worth your limited time and resources to market to an entire community for the sake of reaching your snowflake consumer.

Defining your audience is also essential because as you may already know, once you have a defined your group of interest and best possible marketing opportunities, you can now begin to target that audience with your branding. This can mean running ads in media that you know members of your key demographic are likely to tune in to, as well as deciding to research the ways in which you can better serve the people who will hopefully become your financial supporters. Let us say, for example, that you are targeting men and women in their 30's and 40's who are interested in cooking. You create a cooking channel on YouTube and write a weekly blog about all things happening in the kitchen. Since you know who will be most likely to tune into your channel, read your blogs, and follow you on social media, you should consider what kinds of things people in this age range and demographic enjoy most. Your recipes are made from simple ingredients and sometimes premade things, so you know that your target audience is most likely people who work and do not have a great deal of time or money to spend on every meal, but still want to make them taste good and be nutritious. You could write several posts periodically about the importance of balancing time with quality preparation in the kitchen. You could make sure to use less professional techniques and make your videos easy to follow and recreate at home. You could partner with brands that are available in the lesser-expensive grocery stores when sponsoring products or having videos paid for.

Ultimately, defining your audience will help you to conduct a better, more targeted effort in your personal brand, and it simply involves identifying your audience, then getting to know them and the things that they value, then implementing that into your branding technique. You can even cater to your audience without compromising yourself in professional branding. Yes, it is somewhat more difficult to know what a potential employer wants as they do not publish market research reports on such things, but you can deduce what type of things they are looking for simply by getting to know more about the company. Read their website and memorize their company values. If you have the time, prior to an interview or submitting a resume, include some of those keywords into your social media posts. See what kinds of coworkers they have hired. Are there any common traits you see? Get to know what your potential employer wants to see and hear from an ideal candidate, and do your best to implement that into your own brand and delivery. Defining your audience is simply identifying who is most likely to buy what you are branding, and then giving them what they would like most. Learn to empathize with your audience and make them feel comfortable when taking in everything you have to offer.

Chapter Seven: Personal Branding with Facebook

Personal branding on Facebook is key, no matter what your ultimate goals for personal branding are. In order to build your brand on Facebook, you will have to first create a personal account. If you already have one, then you can simply revamp it under the following guidelines.

- ✓ Make your profile picture clean and professional- NO SELFIES OR MIRROR SHOTS. It is a good idea to invest in some professional pictures in multiple outfits from a real photographer and have them sent to your computer.

- ✓ Choose a color scheme, as well as a background or 'banner' photo that perfectly encapsulates the 'feeling of you'. Example: if your brand is focused on clean living and exercise, choose a stock photo of exercise equipment, a counter full of fruits and vegetables, etc...Make it relevant, clean, and not too specific

- ✓ Begin posting pictures and messages daily, if not multiple times a day. Clear pout any personal photos you already have on your account, no matter how personal. You want your page to appear professional and curated, not as if you are just another random person. Post clean, interesting photos of yourself and, if relevant, your loved ones. Refrain from personal messages to friends or family on your page- only things relating to your brand should go on your homepage

- ✓ Create interesting content by posting inspirational memes, links to articles related to your brand, make videos and do live streams

- ✓ Connect with others related to your field, join groups to get yourself known

- ✓ Pictures of yourself can be dramatic, sexy (within reason), artsy, relevant, advertisements, pics of you smiling, laughing or fun candid pictures.

- ✓ Pictures of yourself cannot be: selfies, blurry, with poor lighting, in street clothes, with un-styled hair or makeup, controversial, political or religious (unless your brand is involved with politics or religion), advertised without saying they are advertisements

If this is your first time making a Facebook page, then you need to recruit friends, and fast. Search for anyone you know and begin reaching out to them on Facebook and hope that they friend you back. You could even get out old yearbooks and go name by name. You will not be using this account for personal reasons so security is not an issue. The more friends you have the more popular you seem, so get your friend count higher quickly.

If you have a business component to your brand, such as our example John who was selling his artwork, you also need to create a business Facebook page. Curate it in a similar way to your personal account, only with more pictures of your work or product. From here, you can create ads and 'boost posts' to targeted demographics and audiences and have them run for specific days to attract more buyers and generate more word of mouth for your brand. Be sure to include a picture of yourself in your post! This may be the first time people see your brand, so use interesting, clear and crisp photos.

Chapter Eight: Personal Branding on Instagram

Personal branding on Instagram is very similar to branding on Facebook. You will need to follow all of the previous guidelines for how to create an account or clear out your current account. If Instagram is your main vessel for storing pictures, consider creating a new account and changing the name on your current account to a nickname or something else people would recognize you by so your full name can be used for your personal brand. You could even consider coming up with a cool and relevant nickname for your brand if you desire.

With Instagram, however, you will be in search of followers, and unlike like Facebook, Instagram does not have a friend request option. Followers are only brought to you if THEY want to follow you, regardless of whether or not you follow them. So try reaching out to friends and family in real life and asking them to follow you. Then the people who follow them will see your profile in their recommendations. You could also create an ad for your account on Instagram. However, it must be a business page and you must also have a Facebook business page to do so. Once you do, however, you will have five different options for creating and running an ad, including photos, videos, conversions, and outreach. Each ad is tailored to a demographic and unlike Facebook, you cannot ignore Instagram ads, as you have to scroll past them in order to see more photos on your page. Instagram stars garner big followings by creating very interesting content such as videos in under 60 seconds, and their followers share their videos across other platforms. Encourage those you know and your followers to share your content so that you can reach more people, and remember the picture guidelines from chapter seven!

Chapter Nine: Personal Branding on YouTube

YouTube is a video publishing platform that, while many of us have accounts on, not many of us publish videos there. Even if you do not want a career based on YouTube, you can still use it to your advantage for advancing your personal brand. When creating videos, make sure they are well lit, have clear sound, and edited well. Search for video editing software that will fit your budget and computer operating system requirements. Make a unique and styled channel page with color schemes, fonts, and relevant pictures. Create a short video introducing your channel and telling people about the video you'll be posting to it and why. From then on, publish videos at least once every week, preferably on the same day and time, if not more often. While the specifics of videos you make will vary depending on your personal brand, you can always be sure that your content does not include swear words, sexual content, or immoral actions or you could face demonetization, wherein you will not make money off of your videos. Anyone with a YouTube account and the funds can create ads to get your video more views, which do not count until the viewer has watched for at 30 seconds. Try connecting with other YouTube stars as they are a close-knit community and often collaborate together and support each other.

Chapter Ten: Personal Branding with Twitter

Twitter is the least customizable yet somehow most personal of all social media platforms. You can create an account using your nicest profile picture and can choose a background image for your page. However and pictures you post will only be listed as a hyperlink in your text body, and can be viewed only as part of an album featured on your page. Twitter is best used, then, for sending out thoughts, messages, and links to other relevant materials or content. Twitter is fast and simple to use, although it is still recommended you clear out all of your old tweets so your new or revamped account is seemingly professional. Try and share only positive thoughts and comments, or things only relevant to your brand. People's biggest source of unease and bitterness in 2019 is reading hurtful or negative things online, so refrain from posting such things on your accounts. Send out tweets regularly with reminders of upcoming events or projects, and you can even 'live-tweet' events and inform followers of how things are going. Try to use professional but familiar language, and start off by again recruiting the people you know to follow you. Try following random strangers and see if they will follow you back. You can create ads on Twitter to boost the audience of who sees your post, but it will be pinned as 'promoted' when people see it so they will know it was paid for. Avoid getting into rants, fights, or long-standing feuds with people to avoid looking divisive, and be sure to follow the picture and video guidelines set forth in previous chapters.

Chapter Eleven: Having Mentorships

A mentor is an essential part of the personal branding process. A mentor is someone who will help to guide you through the highs and lows of the personal branding journey, giving you key pieces of advice and resources. At this point you may be asking yourself 'Ok, but how on Earth do I find one?". Basically, a mentor is an experienced professional in your field who has built their own successful personal brand or has been the working force behind the personal brand of someone else. While anyone with a successful personal branding career will be a great resource of help and guidance for you, typically you should begin the search for a mentor by looking at people with careers and results similar to what you want to achieve. For example, if you wanted to create a food based YouTube channel, you could reach out to the creator of the popular channel Binging With Babish. Not only does he has millions of followers, but he has also created a unique and easy to follow set up and is one of the few YouTube stars who is consistent with video delivery dates. Many personal brands have professional business emails attached to them, either featured on their website, in video descriptions, or on social media biographies. It is a good idea to contact a wide range of possible mentors, as chances are that anyone with a successful full-force personal brand is going to be busy and unable to respond to you. Try contacting at least 50 people, and although you may want to have a Martha Stewart level career, do not waste your time reaching out to any celebrities. Contact lesser-known authors, video creators, etc...as they will be more likely to help you. A great portion of finding a mentor is trying to connect to people's heartstrings and hope that they will see your talent and value your vision enough to take the time to help you.

Having a mentor is also quite possible, and perhaps even easier to find, when you are seeking to build yourself a personal brand solely in the realm of a professional career. You can take the time to research other working professionals who perhaps have the job that you are hoping to get, or perhaps have an even higher or more coveted position. These professionals could be found online by searching through company directories on websites or even looking through profiles on LinkedIn. Again, you will want to reach out to multiple people as some may not respond to you, however, the chances are much more likely that they will, even if it is just to thank you for your time and tell you they are unavailable. If you do receive multiple offers to guide you, however, take hold of every opportunity. Chances are that most mentors will not be staying in your life for a long period of time, so be willing to stretch yourself thin for a short period of time in order to absorb the most knowledge and wisdom from those who have made it to where you want to be. Once you have one, or even several, experienced people willing to give you their time and attention, it may feel overwhelming or confusing as to what to ask them. So start out by creating an interview style list of questions, wherein you ask anyone who is willing to help you the same set of rudimentary questions, such as "How did you accomplish this?", "What technology do you use?", or "How long did this take?". You may find different answers than you expected, and it will begin to give you a more accurate gauge of what you can expect going into the process of building a personal brand or yourself. Ultimately, your mentor will someone you can keep in your life to ask all of the questions you may find you need to be answered along the way, and with any luck, they will admire your tenacity and courage and will do their best to help you succeed.

Chapter Twelve: How to Monitor Your Personal Brand

You have now created multiple social media accounts, set realistic goals, and have started to market yourself and what you have to offer the world. You have contacted valuable people and gathered the resources you will need to succeed. You have begun creating content and have found a receptive audience for what you are doing. Your main focus now is to achieve the goals that you have set in a timely manner and to start bringing in revenue through one of the multiple streams, such as creating personal merchandise, sponsoring products, getting ad sponsorships, or receiving views and likes on monetized videos. Now that the wheel of your personal branding journey have started turning and you have found your foundation to be solid, you may be asking yourself where exactly do I go from here? Am I going to be successful or unsuccessful because I do or don't achieve some of my goals? Exactly how do I measure and gauge my success so I can determine whether or not this has all been worth it?

Well, the first step in monitoring the progress of your personal brand is to start by examining the solid numbers you can find across your platforms. On your social media accounts, keep track of the number of followers you have as well as likes and comments. In theory, this number should be growing over the course of your career, seeing higher boosts after things such as collaborations or interviews. Next, you can view the number of views on videos and blog posts, as well as see if people are reading or purchasing other content you have created, such as magazines, books, or online letters. The tangible numbers and how much revenue you are taking in will be the best ways to easily gauge your progress as time goes on. However, there are others ways than numbers to measure your successes. For example, you can factor into the worth of your brand how it makes you feel to be working in the field. Is it much more difficult and stressful than you thought, or do you enjoy your work on a daily basis? You can also consider how many resources you have put into your efforts and how many resources you are receiving in return. Are you at a substantial loss, are you making a profit, or are you breaking even? Just as with any business, you need to know the answer to this question at any given time and need to make changes if the results are not what you would like for them to be.

You can also monitor the success of your personal brand by assessing how many new opportunities you are able to get over the course of your career. Are you being approached to sell or endorse products, or are you being asked to do collaborations? Have you gotten the attention of publishers or other influential people in your field of work or in the media? If the answer is no, perhaps you can begin rethinking your strategy and start working to actively garner more opportunities for publicity and revenue. If you were only personal branding for the sake of bettering your job opportunities or promotions, then your progress can be monitored by simply whether or not you got those new opportunities. It is very important that, regardless of what level of branding you are pursuing, that you actively ensure you are maintaining your social accounts and other outlets as those who post infrequently lose followers and therefore lose opportunities. Ultimately, monitoring your brand is simply asking yourself the questions of where you think you ought to be by now, and then actually reviewing where you are and gauging how well the two line up. If they do not, you now know you need to change your methodology and approach. If they do, you know that you need to continue doing what works and work towards creating an even better career. A good idea is to have these 'check-ins' periodically, and how often they occur is really up to you, though anything more than once a month is unnecessary. Monitoring your brand is essentially checking in with your career so that you can tailor the results of your work to fit the needs of your life.

Conclusion

Thank for making it through to the end of *Personal Branding in 2019*, and let's hope it was informative and able to provide you with all of the tools you need to achieve your goals whatever it is that they may be. Just because you've finished this book doesn't mean there is nothing left to learn on the topic, and expanding your horizons is the only way to find the mastery you seek.

The next step is to begin researching other successful personal brands and why they interest you. Take the time to get an understanding of why they are successful. Then go on to complete the personal branding foundation checklist, realizing what you have to offer the world and how you can utilize what makes you unique and valuable to begin a long and fulfilling career.

Continue to research possible mentors and idols, as well as new or innovative techniques and brands that you could admire and incorporate into your own efforts. Remember to take an honest and accurate gauge of the resources that are available to you, and use them with care and responsibility. When beginning to build your personal brand, remember to always be yourself and make an active and purposeful effort to curate a unique, styled, and marketable brand and image that will sell your persona and skills. No one else can be Martha Stewart, and no one else can be YOU.

Finally, if you found this book useful in any way, a review on Amazon is always appreciated!

www.ingramcontent.com/pod-product-compliance
Lightning Source LLC
Chambersburg PA
CBHW030938240526
45463CB00015B/396